Ten Poems
about Aunts

ex libris

Candlestick Press

Published by:
Candlestick Press,
DiVersity House, 72 Nottingham Road,
Arnold, Nottingham NG5 6LF
www.candlestickpress.co.uk

Design, typesetting, print and production by Diversity Creative
Marketing Solutions Ltd., www.diversitymarketing.co.uk

Cover illustration: © Amy Blackwell 2013, www.amyblackwell.co.uk
Introduction and selection: © Anne Harvey, 2013

ISBN 978 1 907598 17 3

This pamphlet is dedicated to all aunts, the world over.

Our thanks to Anne Harvey, who found these poems and whose lovely idea
this pamphlet was.

Thanks are also due to

Christine Webb for 'Aunt Em' © Christine Webb, from *After Babel*,
(Peterloo Poets, 2004); David Higham Associates for permission to reprint
both 'Aunt Sue's Stories' by Langston Hughes, from *Collected Poems of
Langston Hughes* (Alfred A Knopf Inc., 1994) and 'Dora' by
Charles Causley, from *Collected Poems 1951-2000* (Picador, 2000).
'Aunts' by Virginia Graham is reprinted from *Consider the Years*
(Persephone Books, 2000), www.persephonebooks.co.uk , 'The Niece',
by Martin Armstrong, is reprinted by permission of Peters Fraser & Dunlop
(www.petersfraserdunlop.com); 'A House of Mercy' by Stevie Smith, from
Collected Poems of Stevie Smith (Penguin, 1972), is reproduced by
permission of James & James Publishers, Executors of the Estate of James
MacGibbon; 'Aunt Julia' by Norman MacCaig, from *The Poems of Norman
MacCaig* (Polygon, 2009), is reprinted by permission of the Estate of
Norman MacCaig.

Where poets are no longer living, their dates are given.

Introduction

'There is something in the relationship between Aunts and their nephews and nieces that is quite unlike any other,' wrote essayist Robert Lynd adding, 'Looking back I can see that there is nothing but good to be said of aunts'.

As an aunt myself I find that very encouraging, especially as aunts often get a very raw deal in literature. Tony Lumpkin in Goldsmith's comedy *She Stoops to Conquer* says, 'To be sure Aunts of all kinds are damned bad things' and it seems that Richmal Crompton's William Brown and P. G. Wodehouse's Bertie Wooster would agree with him. Some very judgemental, tight-fisted and quite extraordinary aunts appear in these books, and are matched by countless other gorgons such as Lady Bracknell in *The Importance of Being Ernest* and the dreaded Aunt Reed in *Jane Eyre*.

The aunts of my childhood are well-remembered: Big Auntie Bessie, who liked to warm her backside at the fire, lifting her skirt... snobby Auntie Constance, who liked to buy even her buttons in Harrods... Great Aunt Ada, who however lavish the set tea-table always found something missing. In the words ending Virginia Graham's warm and loving tribute, all those 'nigh-forgotten, soon-remembered aunts'.

Anne Harvey

To Auntie

'Chief of our Aunts', not only I,
But all your dozen nurslings cry -
'What did the other children do?
And what were childhood, wanting you?'

Robert Louis Stevenson (1850 – 1894)

Aunt Em

There was Aunt Em. She was earth mother:
baked her own bread, made porridge
lemoncurd gravy biscuits
sewed worn sheets sides to middle
gave her youngest sister hints about
sex, sang contralto in the chapel. Shirts
and china rose brilliant from her soap-foamed
hands, more gnarled each year. She sat down
seriously in the library, choosing
her books with pursed lips, nodding
at her pencilled list, the fragile bun
of her hair quivering, skewered
with pins. Fifty years she ruled
kitchen and family with loving
labour and sharp-eyed reproof. I see her
eternally brandishing the blade
of the handle-less breadknife, making a point
in some argument, as she cut the bread
on returning from chapel, with her hat still on.

Christine Webb

Aunts

Children, when you have gone your several ways,
and have sought the long days'
happiness, and the night's elusive dream,
incredible as it may seem
you will turn, at some moment, like thirsting plants
to your aunts.
  Now, aunts are not glamorous creatures,
as very often their features
tend to be elderly caricatures of your own.
Aunts use eau-de-cologne
and live in rather out-of-the-way places,
and wear pointed white shoes with laces
tied in a neat bow.
  Oh, I know, I know!
  Nevertheless I maintain
that when you are old enough to learn pain,
are acquainted with sorrow, and know what fear is,
your aunts will not seem nearly such drearies.
  You'll see,
believe me!
  When you've broken off your engagement and want to hide,
you will go to Aunt Beatrice at Ambleside.
When the charwoman falls down dead,
Aunt Edith will give you a bed.
When your heart breaks, as hearts sometimes do,
Aunt Constance at Looe
will feed it on Cornish cream and philosophy,
soothe it with strawberries for tea;
and when, with the dew still behind your ears
you set forth to conquer wider spheres,
I do not think you will get much further the first night
than Aunt Maud in Shanklin, Isle of Wight.

Oh, yes, children, aunts are kind
and quite resigned
to the fact that you will not go near them for years,
and then bring them your tears.
Although at your tender age
you resent their neglect of the Stage,
their inability to differentiate between jazz and swing,
and their poor reactions to Bing,
the day will dawn when they will rise up like rocks,
sheltering you with their long imprimé frocks
and cornflowered hats worn at such hopeless slants –
your nigh-forgotten, soon-remembered aunts.

Virginia Graham (1910 – 1993)

A House of Mercy

It was a house of female habitation,
Two ladies fair inhabited the house,
And they were brave. For although Fear knocked loud
Upon the door, and said he must come in,
They did not let him in.

There were also two feeble babes, two girls,
That Mrs S. had by her husband had,
He soon left them and went away to sea,
Nor sent them money, nor came home again
Except to borrow back
Her Naval Officer's Wife's Allowance from Mrs S.
Who gave it him at once, she thought she should.

There was also the ladies' aunt
And babes' great aunt, a Mrs Martha Hearn Clode,
And she was elderly.
These ladies put their money all together
And so we lived.

I was the younger of the feeble babes
And when I was a child my mother died
And later Great Aunt Martha Hearn Clode died
And later still my sister went away.

Now I am old I tend my mother's sister
The noble aunt who so long tended us,
Faithful and True her name is. Tranquil.
Also Sardonic. And I tend the house.

It is a house of female habitation
A house expecting strength as it is strong
A house of aristocratic mould that looks apart
When tears fall; counts despair
Derisory. Yet it has kept us well. For all its faults,
If they are faults, of sternness and reserve,
It is a Being of warmth I think; at heart
A house of mercy.

Stevie Smith (1902 – 1971)

Aunt Julia

Aunt Julia spoke Gaelic
very loud and very fast.
I could not answer her —
I could not understand her.

She wore men's boots
when she wore any.
— I can see her strong foot,
stained with peat,
paddling the treadle of the spinningwheel
while her right hand drew yarn
marvellously out of the air.

Hers was the only house
where I lay at night
in the absolute darkness
of the box bed, listening to
crickets being friendly.

She was buckets
and water flouncing into them.
She was winds pouring wetly
round house-ends.
She was brown eggs, black skirts
and a keeper of threepennybits
in a teapot.

Aunt Julia spoke Gaelic
very loud and very fast.
By the time I had learned
a little, she lay
silenced in the absolute black
of a sandy grave

At Luskentyre.
But I hear her still, welcoming me
with a seagull's voice
across a hundred yards
of peatscrapes and lazybeds
and getting angry, getting angry
with so many questions
unanswered.

Norman MacCaig (1910 – 1996)

Dora

My last aunt, Dora Jane, her eye shrill blue,
The volted glance, the flesh scrubbed apple-clean,
Bullets for fingers, hair cut like a man,
Feet in a prophet's sandals, took the view
That work was worship; kept a kitchen share
In this her book of very common prayer.

She never called me Charles. Instead, the name
My father went by: Charlie. Who brought home
The war stowed in his body's luggage; died
In nineteen twenty-four. The strong wound bled
Unspoken in her heart, no signal tear
Disburdened on a waywardness of air.

One tale she prised from childhood. Prised again.
A brother and two sisters. How they ran
To the high field, through the tall harvest sea,
The stolen matches for a summer game.
As it was born, each pretty painted flame
Matching the sun's fire. And how suddenly

The youngest was a torch, and falling, falling,
Swathes of her long hair, and her burned voice calling.
Indifferent, the sun moved down the day:
The boy, my father, beating hand to bone
On the hard flame that struck a breath away
And turned a body and blood to a black stone.

Caught in her trap of years, Dora still told
Her tale, unvarying as granite. Held
Life at arm's length. And there were lovers, though
The clear blue gaze killed questioning. Revered
The tarot pack, fortunes in tea-cups. Feared
Nothing when it was time for her to go;

Half-smiled at me as a sentimentalist.
The biscuit-tin clock thumping by her bed
Placed so that she could see the day drawl by.
Our only death, said Dora, is our first.
And she turned from me. But her winter eye
Spoke every word that I had left unread.

Charles Causley (1917 – 2003)

Aunt Sue's Stories

Aunt Sue has a head full of stories.
Aunt Sue has a whole heart full of stories.
Summer nights on the front porch
Aunt Sue cuddles a brown-faced child to her bosom
And tells him stories.

Black slaves
Working in the hot sun,
And black slaves
Walking in the dewy night,
And black slaves
Singing sorrow songs on the banks of a mighty river
Mingle themselves softly

In the flow of old Aunt Sue's voice,
Mingle themselves softly
In the dark shadows that cross and recross
Aunt Sue's stories.

And the dark-faced child, listening,
Knows that Aunt Sue's stories are real stories.
He knows that Aunt Sue never got her stories
Out of any book at all,
But that they came
Right out of her own life.

The dark-faced child is quiet
Of a summer night
Listening to Aunt Sue's stories.

Langston Hughes (1902 – 1967)

The Niece

Miss Prudence, careless of her name,
Allowed Jim Sykes, her latest flame,
To lure her to the Dog and Duck;
And there it chanced, by sheer ill-luck,
Her Aunt, Miss Emma Apsley-Bing,
Rather a go-ahead old thing,
Had just popped in, resolved to pry,
With modest but observant eye,
And so discover what the blazes
People *do* inside these places,
And there among the glass and glitters
She sat enjoying gin-and-bitters.
Spying her niece she muttered 'Gee!
How very awkward this will be!
No sociological explanation
Will ever meet the situation.'
And, feigning not to notice Prue,
She racked her brains for what to do.
Miss Prudence, leaning on the bar,
(You know what these young people are),
Fell, as she spotted Auntie Emma,
Into a similar dilemma;
For 'Fancy meeting *you* in here!'
Would gall the sensitive old dear,
While 'Auntie, have the next on me!'
Might fail to strike the proper key.
And so, with perfect coolness, backed
By worldly wisdom and a tact
For which too much cannot be said,
They simply cut the other dead.

But now, whene'er they chance to chat
Of that and this and this and that,
They stare into each others' eyes
Furtively, with a wild surmise.

Martin Armstrong (1882 – 1974)

Aunt Maud

I had written to Aunt Maud
Who was on a trip abroad,
   When I heard she'd died of cramp -
   Just too late to save the stamp.

Aunt Bertha

Oh, gloomy, gloomy was the day
When poor Aunt Bertha ran away!
But Uncle finds to-day more black:
Aunt Bertha's threatening to run back!

Appreciation

Auntie, did you feel no pain
   Falling from that apple tree?
Will you do it, please, again?
   'Cos my friend here didn't see.

Harry Graham (1874 – 1936)